POMPEII TODAY: A MUSEUM OF PEOPLE BURIED ALIVE

ARCHAEOLOGY QUICK GUIDE
CHILDREN'S ARCHAEOLOGY BOOKS

BABY PROFESSOR
EDUCATION KIDS

Speedy Publishing LLC

40 E. Main St. #1156

Newark, DE 19711

www.speedypublishing.com

Copyright 2017

Pompeii was a flourishing city south of Rome. Then, in 79 CE, it was destroyed and buried by an eruption of Mount Vesuvius. Now you can visit Pompeii and see how people lived almost two thousand years ago! Let's find out what we can see on our visit to Pompeii.

THE RISE OF POMPEII

Pompeii was a city in a good location on the west coast of Italy. The first settlements there date back to at least 800 BCE.

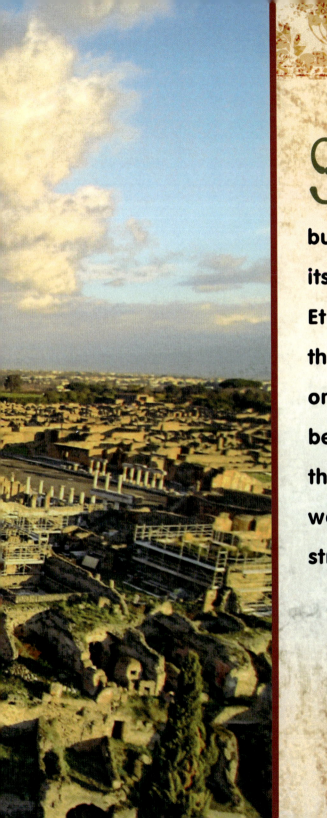

Sometime in the sixth century BCE the city of Pompeii was founded, but we are not sure which people were its first residents. It might have been Etruscans, Greeks, Oscans, or one of the many other cultures that flourished on the Italian peninsula before Rome became powerful enough to dominate the whole area. Whoever the founders were, they built a walled city, with streets laid out in a grid plan.

Sometime in the fourth century BCE Rome extended its control over the communities along the Bay of Naples, including Pompeii. During the war with Carthage, 218-201 BCE, Pompeii joined in efforts to repel the Carthaginian army under Hannibal that had invaded Italy. After Hannibal was defeated, Pompeii continued to grow and prosper; however, it still had an uneasy relationship with Rome.

HANNIBAL IN ITALY

MAP OF POMPEII

In the so-called Social War from 91 to 87 BCE, when the "associate" cities like Pompeii fought against Roman control, Pompeii was attacked and put under siege. After Rome's victory it established a Roman colony in Pompeii, displacing many of the original residents. From then on, Pompeii was a full part of the Roman Republic and then the Roman Empire.

VOLCANO AND DESTRUCTION

Mount Vesuvius stands just a few miles inland from Pompeii. It is an active volcano, but had not erupted since before Rome was founded, so nobody felt like it was a threat. There were farms and vineyards on the slopes of the volcano!

THE INAUGURATION OF THE NEW RAILWAY CONSTRUCTION IN NAPLES IN 1839

In 62 CE there was a heavy earthquake in the region, a warning of instability. But people rebuilt damaged parts of Pompeii and nearby cities without thinking about what might lie ahead. Pompeii continued to grow and expand. It had a year-round population of about 12,000 people, with many summer visitors enjoying seaside holidays away from the heat of Rome.

Then, in the summer of 79 CE, Vesuvius erupted after months of warnings. Many people had already left Pompeii. Those still in town were killed by a combination of a shock wave from the eruption, heat, and poisonous gases the volcano spewed out, and then the whole city was buried under many feet of soot, ash, pumice, and lava from the volcano. Read more about that terrible time in the Baby Professor book *What Happened to Pompeii?*

ERUPTION OF MOUNT VESUVIUS

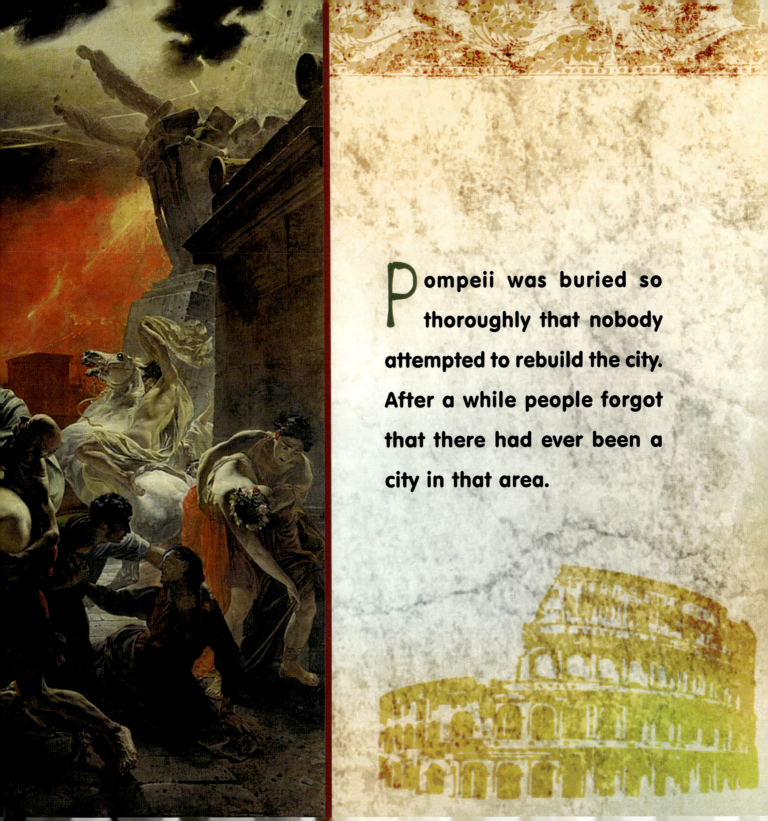

Pompeii was buried so thoroughly that nobody attempted to rebuild the city. After a while people forgot that there had ever been a city in that area.

REDISCOVERING POMPEII

Finally, in 1748, some explorers began to dig down through a thick layer of dust and debris, and discovered the buried city of Pompeii. They were astonished to find that the city was mostly intact. Most of the buildings had not collapsed, and in many houses everything from furniture to plates of food were still in place.

Pompeii now is an amazing way to look at how people lived in the Roman Empire almost two thousand years ago.

As scientists and researchers dug down through the layers of earth and volcanic ash, they found among the streets and buildings odd lumps of material. They discovered these were the layers of fiery ash from the

eruption that had formed around the bodies of the people and animals that died in Pompeii. The outer layer hardened and then preserved the shape of the body within even after everything but the bones had melted away.

GIUSEPPE FIORELLI

In 1863 archaeologist Giuseppe Fiorelli developed a way of preserving the shapes of the bodies by injecting plaster into a mound and letting it harden before breaking away the outer layer of volcanic material.

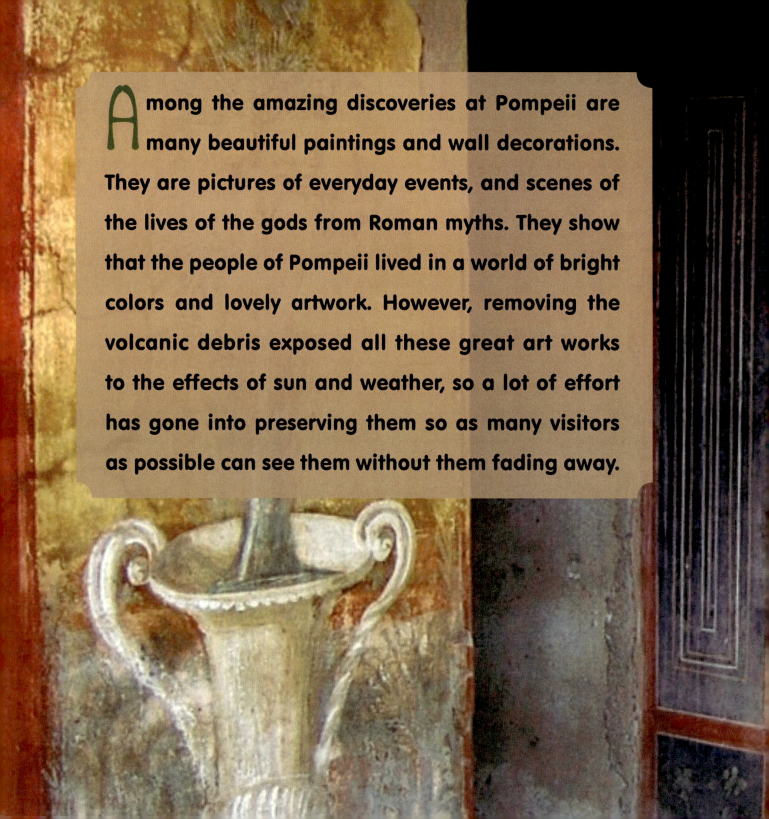

Among the amazing discoveries at Pompeii are many beautiful paintings and wall decorations. They are pictures of everyday events, and scenes of the lives of the gods from Roman myths. They show that the people of Pompeii lived in a world of bright colors and lovely artwork. However, removing the volcanic debris exposed all these great art works to the effects of sun and weather, so a lot of effort has gone into preserving them so as many visitors as possible can see them without them fading away.

MYTHOLOGY WALL PAINTING

In recent times two new efforts have begun. The first is to understand better what the buildings and remains of Pompeii can tell us about how the lives of its citizens connected. How did this house, which was once the home for a great family, become renovated and turn into a bar and fast-food joint for a poor neighborhood? Where did the people live who cleaned the fountains, swept the streets, and delivered the goods to Pompeii's many shops?

BAKERY IN POMPEII

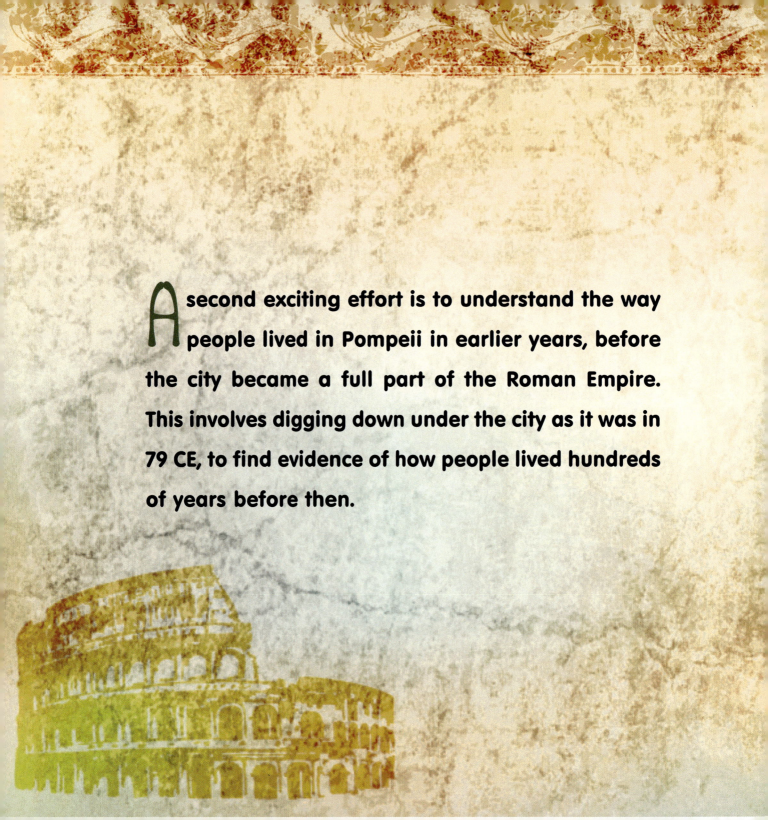

A second exciting effort is to understand the way people lived in Pompeii in earlier years, before the city became a full part of the Roman Empire. This involves digging down under the city as it was in 79 CE, to find evidence of how people lived hundreds of years before then.

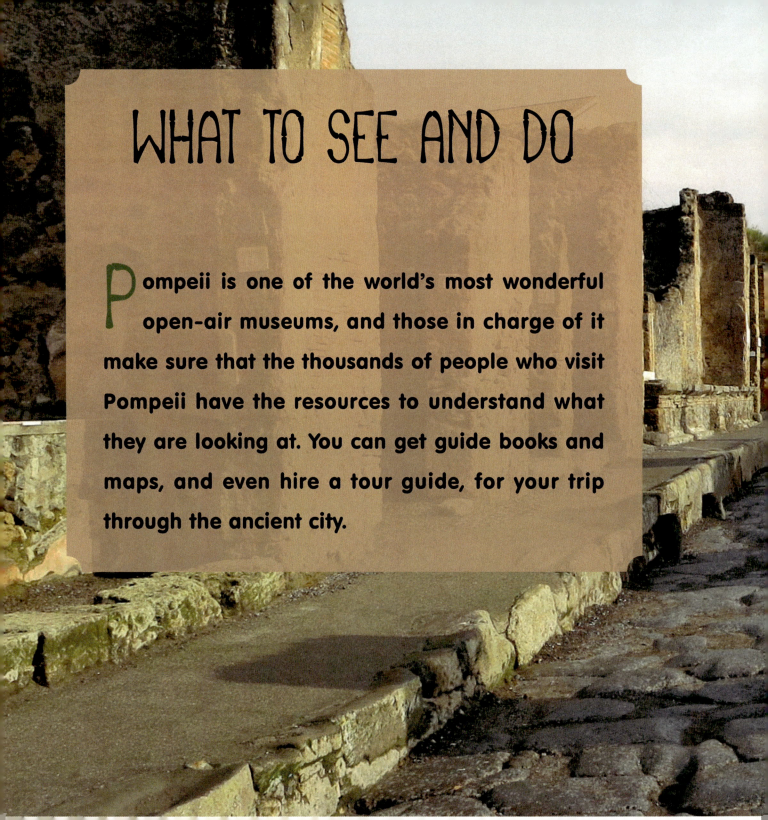

WHAT TO SEE AND DO

Pompeii is one of the world's most wonderful open-air museums, and those in charge of it make sure that the thousands of people who visit Pompeii have the resources to understand what they are looking at. You can get guide books and maps, and even hire a tour guide, for your trip through the ancient city.

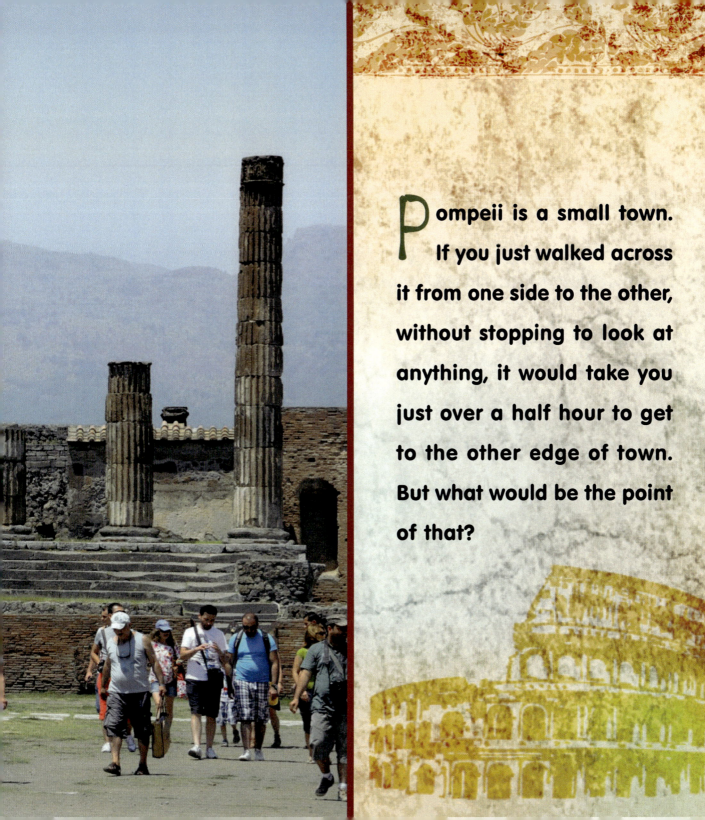

Pompeii is a small town. If you just walked across it from one side to the other, without stopping to look at anything, it would take you just over a half hour to get to the other edge of town. But what would be the point of that?

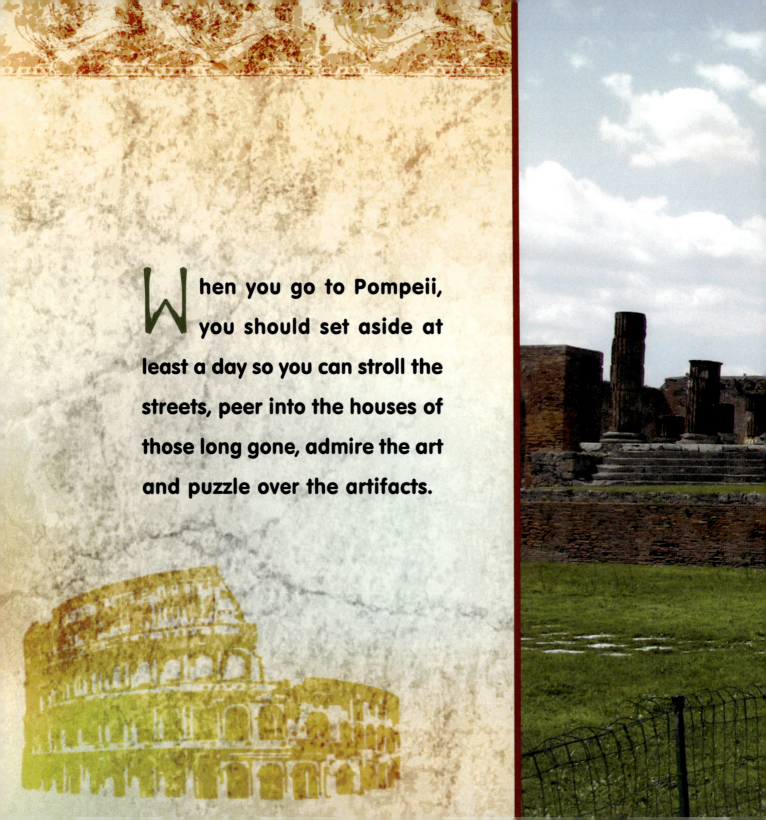

When you go to Pompeii, you should set aside at least a day so you can stroll the streets, peer into the houses of those long gone, admire the art and puzzle over the artifacts.

Even watching the workmen carefully excavating the next building, or restoring an ancient painting, can be a day's entertainment in itself.

As you walk around, remember to watch your step: a lot of the surfaces are uneven. Wear sturdy shoes, take water with you, and plan for regular breaks for meals and to sit and rest, so you don't become too tired or hungry to be able to experience the site.

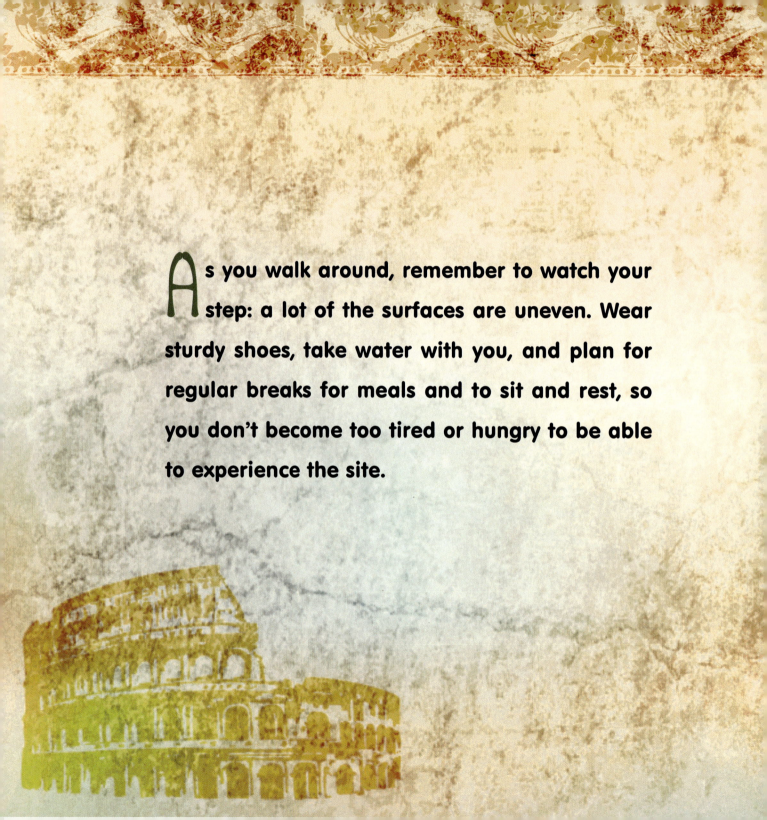

RUINS OF POMPEII

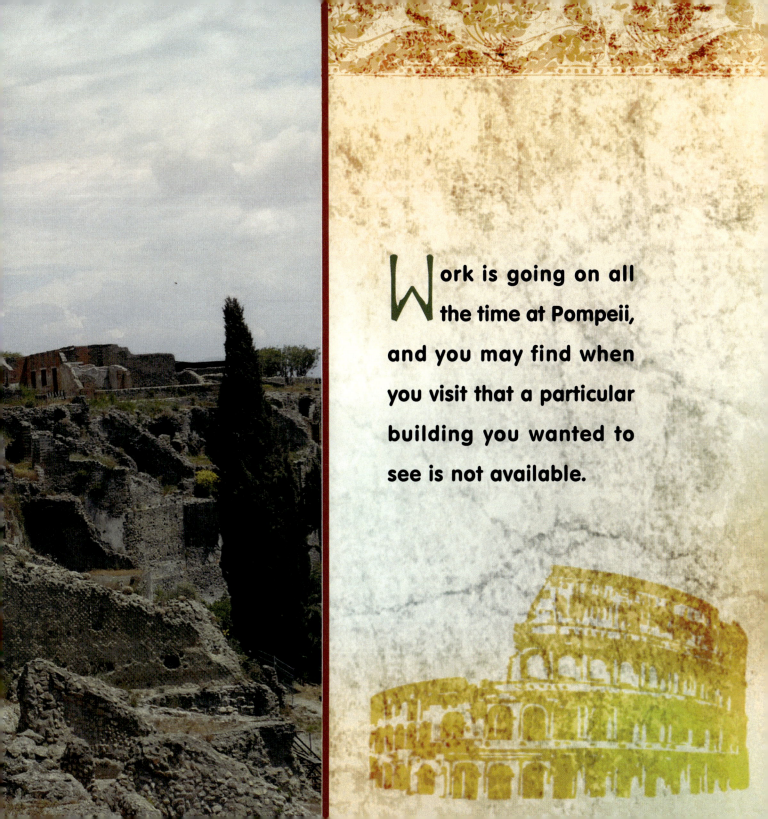

Work is going on all the time at Pompeii, and you may find when you visit that a particular building you wanted to see is not available.

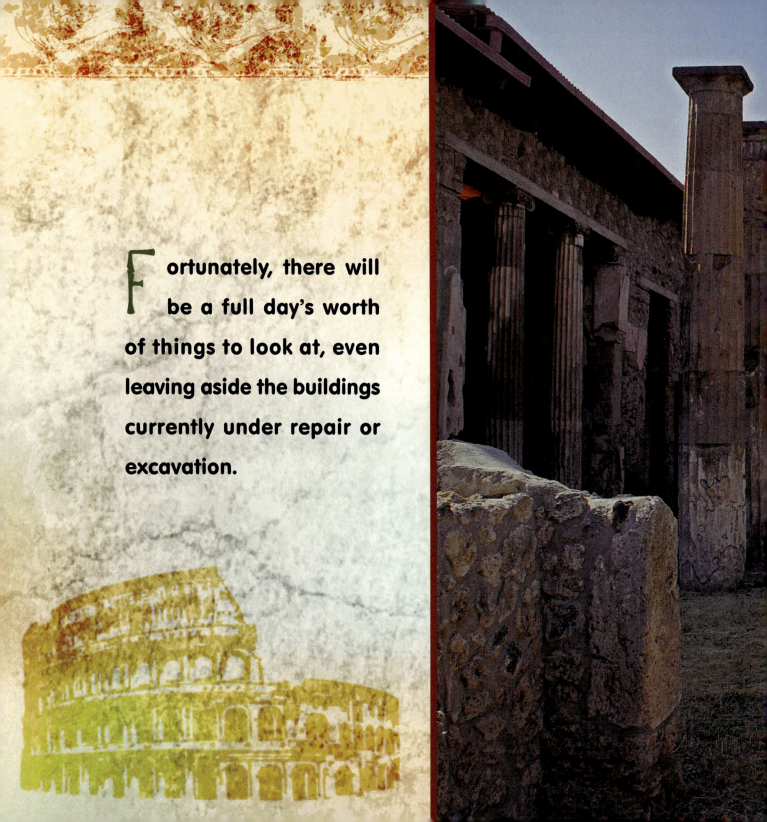

Fortunately, there will be a full day's worth of things to look at, even leaving aside the buildings currently under repair or excavation.

ANCIENT VILLA IN POMPEII

There are maps of Pompeii that use the old Roman way of identifying the buildings by region and by city block. Many of the houses and public buildings also have nicknames, like The House of the Chaste Lovers, that are based on the decorations in the building or the use it was put to.

You can plan your visit using the division of Pompeii into four main areas:

THE HOUSE OF THE CHASTE LOVERS

THE HEART OF THE CITY

Here are the great public buildings like the Forum (the center of city government and the courts), the Basilica, the Temples of Apollo and Jupiter, the

TEMPLES OF APOLLO AND JUPITER

Macellum (the market where people bought and sold food and other goods), and the Building of Eumachia (the headquarters for all the people involved in making cloth goods).

THE BASILICA

BUILDING OF EUMACHIA

This was the "downtown" of Pompeii, and in among the great official buildings are also many small shops, bars, and eating places.

THE ENTERTAINMENT DISTRICT

Not far away is a triangular part of Pompeii which had a smaller forum, temples, theaters, and the buildings where the gladiators lived and trained when they were not involved in public displays of their fighting skills. In ancient times, performances all had a religious aspect, so putting places of worship beside theaters was normal.

ABUNDANCE AVENUE

The Via dell'Abbondanza is a long shopping street, with many interesting attractions down the side streets that lead off it. You can visit the public baths, places where leather-workers processed animal hides into clothing and other goods, grand private homes, an amphitheater for large-scale entertainments, and the brothel where private entertainments of an intimate sort took place. There is also a cemetery and shops of many kinds.

THE NORTH END

There are many grand houses in the north of Pompeii, with attractive nicknames: The House of the Faun, The House of the Ancient Hunt, The House of the Surgeon, and the Villa of the Mysteries.

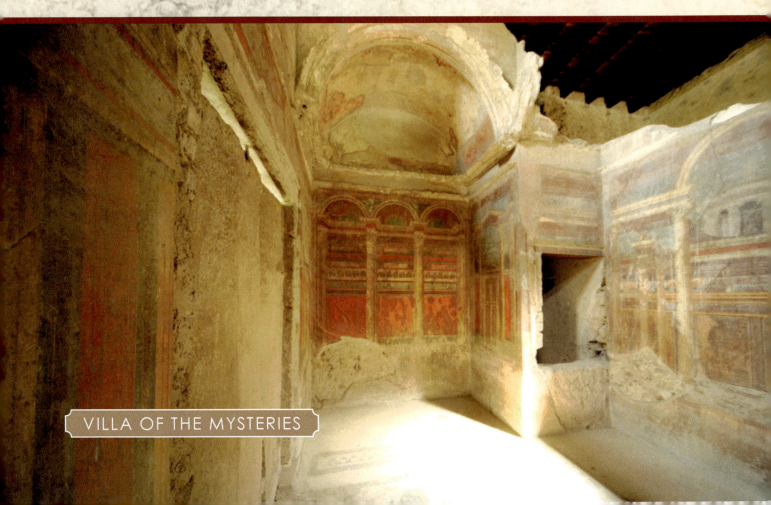

VILLA OF THE MYSTERIES

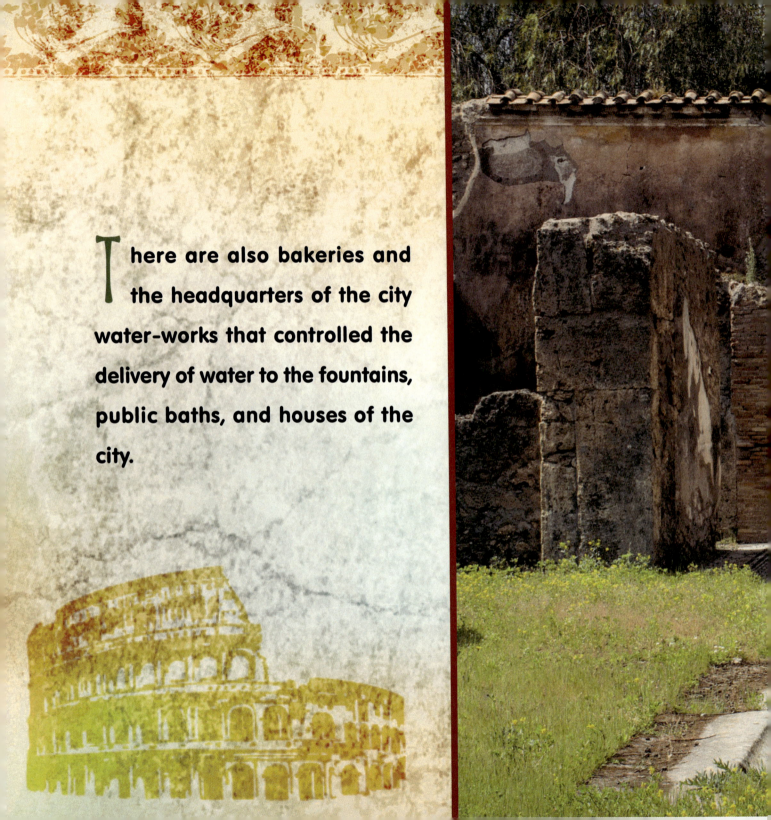

There are also bakeries and the headquarters of the city water-works that controlled the delivery of water to the fountains, public baths, and houses of the city.

DISCOVER MANY ANCIENT WORLDS

People have been building things, from houses to castles to empires, for thousands of years. The remains of their efforts are often available for you to see and learn from. After Pompeii, where will you go? You may get some helpful hints from Baby Professor books like *Who Built the Great Wall of China?*, *The Mayan Cities,* and *Where in the World? Famous Buildings and Landmarks.*

Visit

BABY PROFESSOR
EDUCATION KIDS

www.BabyProfessorBooks.com

to download Free Baby Professor eBooks
and view our catalog of new and exciting
Children's Books

Made in the USA
Las Vegas, NV
30 March 2021